LITURGIES
for
Post-Primary Schools

Brendan Quinlivan

VERITAS

Published 2002 by
Veritas Publications
7/8 Lower Abbey Street
Dublin 1
Ireland

Email publications@veritas.ie
Website www.veritas.ie

Text © Brendan Quinlivan, 2002
Music suggestions © Geraldine Bradley, 2002

ISBN 1 85390 636 0

A catalogue record for this book is available from the British Library.

Veritas books are printed on paper made from the wood pulp of managed forests. For every tree felled, at least one tree is planted, thereby renewing natural resources.

Cover design by Niamh McGarry
Printed in the Republic of Ireland by Criterion Press

CONTENTS

INTRODUCTION

Ritual is part of all our lives. We participate in the rituals of our family and our society to help strengthen our identity as part of those groups. For people involved in the faith formation and development of young people, liturgy and public worship are the rituals we use to re-affirm our relationship with God and God's people. I hope that these texts will give help to religious education teachers, catechists and chaplains who are responsible for the liturgical formation of post-primary students.

Ritual and liturgy can be very effective in the school context and can make a significant contribution to the faith experience of the student. In an ideal world, the liturgies that we celebrate at school should complement the Catholic rituals of parish and family. The reality is that an increasing number of our second level students have less and less experience of ritual outside that which they are offered in the school context.

The liturgies in this book are adaptable and can be altered to suit a particular group. The texts may be used in the context of a Eucharistic celebration or they can stand alone. It is important to use the Scriptures so that our students can hear and read God's word on a regular basis. The language of the texts is religious in style and that is deliberate. Students who study business or technology will learn the vocabulary and linguistic style particular to that subject. Why should religion be any different? A familiarity with religious language will strengthen the link between the school and the parish liturgical life, ensuring that students feel part of the wider faith community.

The keys to effective celebration are preparation and participation. Students should have an opportunity to prepare texts well in advance. A teacher will be able to assign roles in the liturgy that will be mindful of the students' ability. If possible the liturgy should be practised in advance to give the students confidence. This is essential if there is movement or activity included in the liturgy.

I am aware that there is often short notice for a liturgy and I have tried to keep props or accessories that might be needed as simple as possible. Where symbols or gestures are used they will suffer from over-explanation and should be allowed to speak for themselves. Symbols that link us to the wider worshipping community, such as candles, liturgical colours, holy water, the cross, and the bible, should be used all the time. It is important that the liturgy we celebrate be appropriate to the season – for example, we are not at school for Christmas or Holy Week and it would be wrong to celebrate them in anticipation. However, if students have experienced effective celebrations in Advent or Lent then they may look forward to being part of the parish celebration for Christmas and Holy Week along with their families.

Finally can I wish you luck in your endeavours to lead young people in prayer. What you have here is a collection of prayers, notes, photocopies and scribbled ideas that finally have some order put on them. I hope that they will assist you in your work.

Brendan Quinlivan

A NOTE ON THE MUSIC

Music enhances any ritual, especially our religious ones. Today's teachers are fortunate to be working at a time when there is such a wealth of wonderful religious music available. All the suggested material in this book will work well sung in unison with an accompanying instrument (piano or guitar), though some could also be sung unaccompanied/harmonised.

I have limited most of the suggestions to music found in *In Caelo*, which is widely available, and the *Celebration Hymnal for Everyone Vols 1 and 2*. The music of Michael Card is a personal favourite and available on the Internet.

As a teacher, I am very aware that music in some school celebrations is provided by a CD player, and most of this material is also available in that format.

I hope these suggestions will introduce you to some new composers and that you find some new material for your school liturgies.

Geraldine Bradley

MASS FOR THE BEGINNING OF THE SCHOOL YEAR

Scripture texts and music suggestions can be found in the Appendix

GATHERING RITUAL

As the students gather to celebrate the beginning of the New Year in school, some symbols are brought to the altar and presented to invoke God's Blessing on all of the activities that will take place during the year ahead. The commentator reads:

INTRODUCTION

God, our Loving Father, you care greatly for all your children. We want to grow in every way this year closer to you and each other. We stand before you ready to travel further along the road of life and the journey of faith. Help us, and open our hearts to your truth. Bless all our activities in this year ahead so that we may see your plan for us in all that we do.

(Student presents symbol of academic life, e.g. textbook, stationery, etc.)

Bless the work that we do, help us to grow in knowledge and understanding.

(Student presents symbol of sporting life, e.g. football, basketball, hurley, etc.)

Bless the games that we play, help us to grow in strength and fairness.

(Student presents symbol of artistic life, e.g. painting, sculpture, theatre programme)

Bless the things we create, help us to grow in imagination and joy.

(Student presents symbol of the time spent together, e.g. pool cue, game, etc.)

Bless the time we will spend together, help us to grow in harmony and peace.

(Student presents symbol of prayer/religion/faith, e.g. crucifix, bible, rosary, etc.)

Bless the time we spend in prayer, help us to grow in faith, hope and love.

Help us ever loving Father to meet the challenges that this new year will bring. May we see your loving plan for us in all that we undertake and give us the grace to draw closer to you in Christ Jesus Our Lord.

OPENING PRAYER

God of wisdom and understanding, you have guided your people throughout history. Help us to grow in faith and understanding in this coming year. Open our minds to your truth and our hearts to your love that we may grow in wisdom and grace. We ask this through Our Lord Jesus Christ, who lives and reigns with you and the Holy Spirit. One God for ever and ever. Amen.

LITURGY OF THE WORD

FIRST READING

Ecclesiastes 11, 12
Learn wisdom – riches as nothing

RESPONSORIAL PSALM

Psalm 95: 1-2; 3-5
Let us come before the Lord and praise him.

GOSPEL

Matthew 13:44-46
Buried treasure – pearl of great price.

PRAYER OF THE FAITHFUL

PRIEST   All wisdom and understanding is the gift of God. Let us now turn to Him, seeking the gift and graces we need as we begin this new school year.

1. For all students who begin this new year of learning, that they may receive the gifts of wisdom and insight.

2. For all our teachers, that they may share their knowledge in a spirit of gentleness and patience.

3. For all who are denied the right to an education, that they may receive the knowledge and wisdom they need.

4. For all our parents, that their trust and love may always be an example to us.

5. For all who find study or school life difficult, that they may find support in those around them.

6. For all who have died, especially members of our families, past-pupils and teachers of this school, that they may have the fullness of all understanding in the presence of God.

PRIEST   Gracious God, you know our needs even before we ask you. In your great kindness fill us with your wisdom and blessings so that throughout this coming year we may enjoy our learning and delight in new discoveries. Grant this through Christ our Lord. Amen.

LITURGY OF THE EUCHARIST

PRAYER OF THE GIFTS

Father, accept the gifts we offer as we begin this new school year. As this bread and wine is transformed into the body and blood of your Son, help us to grow in knowledge and love of he who lives and reigns for ever and ever. Amen.

COMMUNION RITE

PRAYER AFTER COMMUNION

Lord our God, your spirit fills the earth and teaches us your ways. May the Eucharist we have received nourish and strengthen us as we strive to persevere in our work and in our faith. Grant this through Christ our Lord.

POST-COMMUNION REFLECTION

God, grant me the Serenity
to accept the things
I cannot change,
Courage to change the
things I can,
and the Wisdom
to know the difference.

Living one day at a time;
Enjoying one moment at a time;
Accepting hardship as the
pathway to peace.

Taking, as He did, this
sinful world as it is,
not as I would have it.
Trusting that He will make
all things right if I
surrender to his Will;

That I may be reasonably happy
in this life, and supremely
happy with Him forever in
the next.

Amen

FINAL PROCESSION

Should include the items that symbolised the activities of the forthcoming year – as we have prayed for God's blessing we show that we carry that out from the ceremony into the world.

CHARITY

Scripture texts and music suggestions can be found in the Appendix

SHARING OUR TIME, SHARING OUR TALENT, SHARING OUR TREASURE
(St Vincent de Paul, 27 September)

This liturgy could be celebrated at the conclusion of some practical charitable activity on the part of the students. Students could raise funds for a charitable organisation and present the proceeds in a liturgical context. A representative of the organisation could speak and tell students what difference their efforts will have made to others.

Symbols
1 A timepiece, e.g. clock, representing the time that they have given.
2 Some pages with handprints of each student representing the talent they have used to give a helping hand to others.
3 The money raised from their efforts, e.g. big cheque, etc.
(Symbols should be big/visual and placed in the centre of the assembly.)

GREETING AND INTRODUCTION
(Don't forget to welcome visitors.)

OPENING PRAYER

God our Father, you love us and have been generous to us with your gifts. You give us this world and all we need to live. You give us family and friends who are generous with their love and friendship. Fill us with a spirit of generosity. Help us to see always the people who are in any kind of need. Grant us the courage to respond with our time, our talent and our treasure. We ask this through our Lord Jesus Christ.

READING

> 2 Corinthians 8:1-3, 12
> *They were glad to give generously.*

PSALM

> 103 v. 1, 2 ,5 and 11
> *Response:* The Lord is kind and merciful.

GOSPEL

> Matthew 6:1-4
> *Give in secret and your Father will reward you.*

PRESENTATION OF OFFERINGS

STUDENT 1
(Time)

Charity is about giving of ourselves to others. We are asked by God to make sacrifices so that we can help our brothers and sisters who are in need. This clock reminds us of the time we have. We ask God to help us use our time wisely so that we can all play a part in making the world a better place to live.

STUDENT 2
(Talent)

We all need a helping hand in life. We are loved by the embrace of our family. We are supported by the handshakes of our friends. We are encouraged by the pat on the back that spurs us on to do more. Today we as a class offer a helping hand to those who need it.

STUDENT 3
(Treasure)

True riches do not always come from money. We can sometimes be rich in what we have or own, but be poor in what we share. We offer today from our efforts a contribution to those who need it. May the sharing of our treasure make us rich in friendship and rich in the sight of God.

Contribution can be presented here – representative of group could speak about how the contribution will help.

PRAYERS OF INTERCESSION

LEADER   When we share our time, our talents and our treasure we become closer to those with whom we share and we become closer to God who asks us to share. We turn to him in prayer for all who are in any kind of need.

READER   Our response is: LORD TEACH US TO BE GENEROUS.

1   For all the people who follow Jesus, that they may share their gifts with people in need. We pray to the Lord.

2   For all of us who gather here to pray, that we may grow in generosity and love. We pray to the Lord.

3   For all the people who are in any kind of need, that Jesus will help them through the generosity of other people. We pray to the Lord.

4   *Here include a prayer for the charitable organisation that is being supported.*

5   For all the people who have died, that God may reward their generosity with a place in His kingdom of love. We pray to the Lord.

LEADER   Lord, teach us to be generous, to love and serve you as you deserve, to give and not to count the cost, to fight and not to heed the wounds, to toil and not to seek for rest, to labour and not to seek for any reward save that of knowing we do your holy will. Amen. (*Ignatius*)

Jesus has taught us to pray to God our Father for our daily bread. We now turn to him together, asking that all the material needs of his people will be met.

Our Father ...

CONCLUDING PRAYER

Father of love, you watch over all creation and protect us with your care. Grant that, as we support one another in our need, we may draw ever closer to you in love. We ask this through our Lord Jesus Christ who lives and reigns...

BLESSING

> May God the Father who cares for all his children bless us with time to offer ourselves in generosity. Amen.

> May Jesus Christ who hears the cry of his brothers and sisters in need bless us with talent to help. Amen.

> May God, the Holy Spirit, who fills the hearts of all with love, bless us with treasure to share with others. Amen.

CELEBRATION OF CREATION

Scripture texts and music suggestions can be found in the Appendix

HARVEST, SPRING, GROWTH, NEW YEAR

GREETING AND INTRODUCTION

ACT OF PENITENCE

1   Lord our God, you have given the world to watch over and protect.
     Lord have mercy.

2   Lord, your son has come among us as the light of the world.
     Christ have mercy.

3   Lord our God, your Holy Spirit gives us the power to be light for
     each other, to have courage and remain strong.
     Lord have mercy.

OPENING PRAYER

Good and merciful God, you have given your creation to humanity.
You have put it into our hands so that we might conserve and look
after it. If we take care of this precious gift we can hand it on to our
children in all its beauty. Give us the grace to protect his gift and to
be grateful for the things we receive from the earth. We ask this
through our Lord Jesus Christ. Amen.

READING

Deuteronomy 8:7-10
You will have all you want to eat.

PSALM

Psalm 147:5, 7, 8
Response: Shout praises to the Lord.

GOSPEL

Luke 12:15-21
Life is not made secure by possessions.

HOMILY

Why creation? State of creation today. Responsibility for our environment.
Personal relationship with creation.

CELEBRATION OF NATURE

1   We bring water from (local river/stream/well). It is cold and refreshing. You have created it, O Lord, to serve the needs of all mankind. It refreshed the spirit and gives us an energy for life.

2   We bring a potato. It is small and unattractive. It is dirty because it comes from the earth. You have created it, O Lord, to serve the needs of mankind. It provides us with the nourishment we need and it takes away our hunger.

3   We bring a flower. It is beautiful and colourful. You have created it, O Lord, to serve the needs of all mankind. It brings joy to the spirit which helps us in life.

4   We bring part of a tree. It is solid and strong, planted many generations ago in hope and trust. You have created it, O Lord, to serve the needs of all mankind. It purifies our atmosphere and gives protection to mankind and animals.

5   We bring ourselves. We are all different and individual. You have created us, O Lord, to know, love and serve you. In doing this we will be happy for ever.

PRAYERS OF INTERCESSION

LEADER   We turn in prayer to the Lord our God, who has created us and created the universe.

1   For the Church that it may proclaim and teach faith in God the Creator of all.
Lord hear us.

2   For all of us who gather to pray, that we may grow in knowledge, love and respect for the world around us.
Lord hear us.

3   For all who guide leaders and governments that they may put policies in place that protect and conserve the natural world.
Lord hear us.

4   For those who act in ways that damage and destroy our created world, that they may be converted to see the value of our world.
Lord hear us.

5   For all the gifts that the earth has given us, we give you thanks, O Lord.
Lord hear us.

LEADER   Heavenly Father, you guide all creation towards perfection. We thank you for the world you have created to serve our needs and we offer all our prayers through Christ our Lord. Amen.

Our Father...

CONCLUDING PRAYER

Remain with us, O Lord our God, and help us to know you. We praise you as our creator and as the one who guides our lives. Renew and refresh in us all that you have created and preserve all that you have renewed. We ask this through Christ our Lord. Amen.

May the blessing of Almighty God come down upon us and upon all he has created. The blessing of God the Father, the Son and the Holy Spirit. Amen.

COMMEMORATION OF THE FAITHFUL DEPARTED

Scripture texts and music suggestions can be found in the Appendix

NOVEMBER

This liturgy is suitable for a general remembrance during the month of November. In advance of the service students should have the opportunity to submit the names of people they wish to have remembered. This chance could also be given to students who will not participate in the liturgy. The names can be gathered in any number of ways.

1   *A book called the 'Book of the Living' is placed in a prominent place in the school. It should be a substantial/impressive 'visitors' type book with a strong cover and decorated appropriately. It should be given an important setting with colour/decoration, etc. Students can inscribe the names of deceased family and friends in the book that they wish to have remembered in the liturgy.*

2   *A box is placed somewhere in the school and students can place lists in the box with the names of people they wish to remember. This means that the lists are more private.*

ENTRANCE

The list of faithful departed is brought in procession to a central location in the prayer space. If possible, the book/box is honoured with thurible/incense.

OPENING PRAYER

> Merciful God, you are the Lord of the living and the dead. You give to each one of us the precious gift of memory. When we remember them, those who have died live again in our hearts. Send your Holy Spirit to give us consolation in our loneliness and hope in the eternal life that you promised us through your son, Jesus Christ our Lord. Amen.

LITURGY OF THE WORD

READING

> 1 John 3:1-2
> *We shall see God as he really is.*

PSALM

> Psalm 26
> *The Lord is my light and my help*

GOSPEL

> John 14:1-3
> *Do not let your hearts be troubled*

RITUAL OF REMEMBRANCE

Each of the students is given a night-light which (if possible) is lit from the Easter Candle. The leader explains the significance of the Easter Candle and invites the students to recall the names of special people in their lives whose names they may have already included on their list or in the 'Book of the Living'. Then they can place the night-lights before the book and these can be incensed. This can be done with some quiet background music and at the conclusion a student could read the following:

On the Other Side of Death

Death is a GATEWAY
we all must pass through
to reach that Fair Land
where the soul's born anew.

For man's born to die
And his sojourn on earth
is a short span of years
beginning with a birth...

And like pilgrims we wander
until death takes our hand
and we start on our journey
to God's Promised Land.

A place where we'll find
no suffering nor tears.
Where TIME is not counted.
by days, months or years ...

And in this Fair City
that God has prepared
are unending joys
to be happily shared.

With all of our loved ones
who patiently wait
On Death's Other Side
to open 'THE GATE'.

Helen Steiner Rice
© 1971 The Helen Steiner Rice Foundation
All rights reserved.

INTERCESSIONS

LEADER Loving and merciful God, by raising your son Jesus from the dead you opened the gates of heaven to all who believe in you. Listen to us now as we turn to you in prayer and remember all the people we knew who have died.

1 For all the people we know and love who have died, that they may reach the safety of God's everlasting home. Lord hear us.

2 For all the people who are sad because someone they love has died, that they may receive the help and support they need. Lord hear us.

3 For all of us who have come together to pray, that we may live well and fully in this life, having hope in the life to come. Lord hear us.

4 For people who do not have faith, that they may receive hope from our friendship and support. Lord hear us.

5 For all people who suffer because of old age or illness, that they may have the peace that comes from loving God. Lord hear us.

LEADER Lord, give us the certainty that beyond death there is a life where broken things are mended and lost things are found; where there is rest for the weary and joy for the sad; where all that we have loved and willed of good exists; and where we will meet again our loved ones. We ask this through Christ our Lord. Amen.

BLESSING

Lord, may you support us all day long till the shadows lengthen and evening falls, and the busy world is hushed, and the fever of life is over and our work is done; then in your mercy, Lord, grant us a safe lodging, a holy rest and peace at last.

J.H. Newman

CELEBRATION OF ADVENT

Scripture texts and music suggestions can be found in the Appendix

SEASON OF WAITING, SEARCHING, WELCOME AND RECOGNITION

Use liturgical colours – purple cloths/hangings. Place wreath in a central position. Give the four candles to different students to place in the wreath at appropriate times in the course of the ritual. Only one will be lit during the ritual.

INTRODUCTION

STUDENT

Each year we keep the season of Advent to prepare for the coming of Jesus Christ. Each year is different – another year has passed and we have been changed by our experiences, good and bad, which touch our lives. The world too has changed, war and peace, disasters and new beginnings. We begin this season of winter and the land is asleep but we have hope that spring will come with signs of new life. In this season of Advent we hope in the coming of Jesus Christ who will come with the promise of life and joy.

LEADER

Greeting: Grace, peace and mercy from God our Father to all who prepare their hearts to welcome Jesus who will come into our world.

Response: To Him be glory and praise forever.

STUDENT

Advent is a season of waiting.

Waiting accompanies all of life – it comes before a desire which is incomplete. Waiting is what unites the past, present and future. All of our lives are made up of successive moments, dreams, hopes and, desires. We wait for the seasons to fulfil their promise. We wait for the seed to bring forth its flower. Our waiting is always in hope and in this season of Advent, we wait in joyful hope for the coming of our saviour Jesus Christ. Advent is a season of waiting.

Place first PURPLE candle in wreath.

STUDENT   Advent is a season of searching.

In this season of Advent we search for you, O God. We search for you in the life that we live every day. We search for God in all the things that we do. We search for a joy that will last forever, that comes from knowing Jesus Christ and following his example. God of love, it is you that we search for, even without knowing it. Open our hearts that we may find you in our need.

Place second PURPLE candle in wreath.

STUDENT   Advent is the season of welcome.

When we make someone welcome, we create a bond that is special. As Christians, we believe that when we welcome a stranger, we welcome Jesus into our lives. The friendship that we share is a sign of life. God our Father, we are your guests in this world that you have created. Jesus Christ is your gift to us. Help us to make him welcome in our lives. Advent is a season of welcome.

Place ROSE candle in wreath.

STUDENT   Advent is a season of recognition.

When we recognise someone we are invited to understand them at a deeper level. We recognise someone as a friend sharing with us the gift of themselves. When we recognise someone, there is clarity and understanding. In this season of Advent we recognise God in Jesus Christ who is coming into the world and we recognise Jesus as a brother and friend.

Advent is a season of recognition.

Place third PURPLE candle in wreath.

Leader blesses the wreath.

LEADER   Lord God, we are waiting to celebrate the coming of Jesus into the world. Help us as we search for you in our lives and give us a generous heart that we may make you welcome. Give us the grace to recognise you in our brothers and sisters but most especially in Jesus Christ whose coming we celebrate at Christmas.

Bless this wreath which represents our waiting, our searching, our welcome and our recognition of God's presence in the world.

Leader sprinkles wreath with Holy Water

Student lights first candle.

God of New Beginnings, you have given us your son born into the world as a helpless baby. He is the light of the world, the guiding light we follow in our times of need. May the light of this candle remind us to welcome the Christ-child, that we may follow his example of love, friendship and care.

READING

Luke 12:35-38

See that your lamps are lit.
Waiting for return.
Ready to open door in welcome.

CONCLUDING PRAYER

God, our Father, you loved us so much that you sent your only son into the world to be our saviour and our friend. Grant us your blessing as we wait and search for the coming of your Son. Open our hearts to make him welcome that we may recognise him when he comes. We ask this through Our Lord Jesus Christ who is coming into the world, who lives and reigns with you and the Holy Spirit, one God for ever and ever. Amen.

SERVICE OF RECONCILIATION

Scripture texts and music suggestions can be found in the Appendix

ADVENT SEASON

OPENING PRAYER

Loving God, we gather in this time of advent as we prepare to welcome your Son Jesus Christ into the world. We pray that we might hear your voice and respond to your call to forgive and be forgiven. We come together as people who have sinned. May our time together bring us your forgiveness and help us to see you at work in our everyday lives. We ask this through Christ Our Lord. Amen.

READING

Colossians 3:12-15
Forgive anyone who does you wrong as Christ has forgiven you.

PSALM

Psalm 103:1-2, 3 and 8, 11-12
Response: The Lord is kind and merciful.

GOSPEL

Matthew 3:1-6
Make straight his ways

Homily

The Challenge of Conscience

LEADER   Our conscience challenges us all the time to be the best people we can be. Sometimes we respond to those challenges and surprise even ourselves. From time to time, however, we do not hear the challenge or we ignore it and fail to respond out of fear or selfishness. We listen in quiet time now to the challenges our conscience has made and we ask God's forgiveness for the times we have failed to respond in a generous spirit.

           (These challenges may be changed to suit the age group of the assembly.)

1   I am challenged to know God. I seek forgiveness for the times I have been indifferent or wrapped up in myself, and for the way I have limited my time with God.

2   I am challenged to be just and fair. I seek forgiveness for the times I have not shared my good fortune. I am sorry if my own weakness has allowed me project improper attitudes of racism and intolerance.

3   I am challenged to be a true follower of Jesus. I seek forgiveness for the times that I pretended the gospel message was too difficult to follow and made excuses for not acting in a Christian way.

4   I am challenged to love. I seek forgiveness for any abuse that I may have inflicted or allowed to exist on family members or others in my life, whether it be verbal, emotional, sexual or physical. Help me to heal those whose lives have been broken.

5   I am challenged to believe in myself. I seek forgiveness for the times I have devalued myself before others by the way I have misused my body with food or alcohol or drugs.

6   Mindful of our need for God's sustaining goodness we now approach the priest for your forgiveness and reconciliation.

Individual confession and absolution.

Perhaps a symbol here of the students leaving something with the priest that represents the sins they have left behind.

Our Father...

Exchange of Peace

CONCLUDING PRAYER

God of Mercy, you show us the power of your great love. In forgiving us you give us a freedom to forgive others. As we journey together towards Bethlehem, may we draw closer to you and to one another. We ask this through Christ our Lord. Amen.

A CELEBRATION FOR THE NEW YEAR

Scripture texts and music suggestions can be found in the Appendix

This liturgy might be suitable for the beginning of the calendar year. It could be celebrated on the first week back after the Christmas holidays – probably most suitable for a class who will also be in school the following academic year as it follows the school year in its prayer or symbolism. It's about recognising Christ in the times of our lives. Organise twenty-four students, twelve with candles, twelve with symbols representing the months of the year. When twelve candles are placed they should form a circle representing the continuity and eternity of time.

LEADER   We assemble at the beginning of this new year to dedicate the time ahead to God's care and protection. May all that we begin be done in faith, may all that we undertake be done in hope and may all that we complete be done in love. As we journey through this year it is our prayer that Jesus will accompany us along the way, that we will always be aware of his presence and that we will follow his example of love.

LITURGY OF THE WORD

READING

        Ecclesiastes 3:1-8
        For everything a season

CONSECRATION OF THE YEAR AHEAD

JANUARY

God of New Beginnings, bless us in the month of January – it is the time of new beginnings, the time of resolution, the time of hope. We place our hopes and dreams in the care of our loving God that we may become better people when our hopes and dreams come true.

(Symbol of a SEED is placed)

CANDLEBEARER   Loving God, watch over and protect the light of hope in our lives.

RESPONSE   All times and seasons belong to God.
To God be glory and praise for evermore.

FEBRUARY

God of new life, we bless you in the month of February – it is the time of spring, the time of growth, the time of life. We place our lives in the care of our loving God that we may grow in strength and maturity.

(Symbol of a FLOWER is placed)

CANDLEBEARER   Loving God, watch over and protect the light of growth in our lives.

RESPONSE   All times and seasons belong to God.
To God be glory and praise for evermore.

MARCH

God of faith, we bless you in the month of March – it is the time of St Patrick, the time of St Joseph, the time when God became a human in the womb of Mary. We place our faith in the care of our loving God that we may have a source of strength in our time of need.

(Symbol of a BIBLE is placed)

CANDLEBEARER   Loving God, watch over and protect the light of faith in our lives.

| RESPONSE | All times and seasons belong to God.
To God be glory and praise for evermore. |

APRIL

God of the resurrection, we bless you in the month of April – it is the time of Easter, the time of resurrection, the time of eternal life. We place our eternal souls in the care of our loving God that we may live lives worthy of the promises made to us.

(Symbol of an EVERGREEN is placed)

| CANDLEBEARER | Loving God, watch over and protect the light of eternal life in our lives. |

| RESPONSE | All times and seasons belong to God.
To God be glory and praise for evermore. |

MAY

God of work, we bless you in the month of May – it is the time of study, the time of preparation, the time of perseverance. We place our work and study in the care of our loving God that we may grow in knowledge.

(Symbol of a BOOK is placed)

| CANDLEBEARER | Loving God, watch over and protect the light of learning in our lives. |

| RESPONSE | All times and seasons belong to God.
To God be glory and praise for evermore. |

JUNE

God of wisdom, we bless you in the month of June – it is the time of exams, the time of testing, the time of recall. We place our examinations in the care of our loving God that we may receive the reward of our efforts.

(Symbol of a PEN is placed)

CANDLEBEARER   Loving God, watch over and protect the light of wisdom in our lives.

RESPONSE   All times and seasons belong to God.
To God be glory and praise for evermore.

JULY

God of friendship, we bless you in the month of July – it is the time of holidays, the time of sport, the time of games. We place our friendships in the care of our loving God that we may grow closer to one another.

(Symbol of a FOOTBALL/HURLEY is placed)

CANDLEBEARER   Loving God, watch over and protect the light of friendship in our lives.

RESPONSE   All times and seasons belong to God.
To God be glory and praise for evermore.

AUGUST

God of nature, we bless you in the month of August – it is the time of reaping, the time of harvest, the time of thanksgiving. We place the rewards of our work in the care of our loving God that we may grow in respect for the created world.

(Symbol of WHEAT is placed)

CANDLEBEARER   Loving God, watch over and protect the light of gratitude in our lives.

RESPONSE   All times and seasons belong to God.
To God be glory and praise for evermore.

SEPTEMBER

God of change, we bless you in the month of September – it is the time of return to school, the time of autumn, the time of transition. We place the new opportunities in the care of our loving God that we may grow with every passing year.

(Symbol of a CALENDAR is placed)

CANDLEBEARER   Loving God, watch over and protect the light of change in our lives.

RESPONSE   All times and seasons belong to God.
To God be glory and praise for evermore.

OCTOBER

God of joy, we bless you in the month of October – it is the time of Mary, the time of motherhood, the time of parenthood. We place our parents in the care of our loving God that we may mature in love and respect for all they do for us.

(Symbol of a ROSARY is placed)

CANDLEBEARER   Loving God, watch over and protect the light of joy in our lives.

RESPONSE   All times and seasons belong to God.
To God be glory and praise for evermore.

NOVEMBER

God of all who ever lived, we bless you in the month of November – it is the time of all saints, the time of all souls, the time of remembrance. We place all who have died in the care of our loving God that we may share eternal life with all those we love.

(Symbol of a MASS CARD/MEMORIAL CARD is placed)

CANDLEBEARER   Loving God, watch over and protect the light of memory in our lives.

RESPONSE   All times and seasons belong to God.
To God be glory and praise for evermore.

DECEMBER

God who became man, we bless you in the month of December – it is the time of families, the time of charity, the time of Christ's birth. We place our families in the care of our loving God that we may be people of charity and love.

(Symbol of A CHRISTMAS CARD is placed)

CANDLEBEARER   Loving God, watch over and protect the light of love in our lives.

RESPONSE   All times and seasons belong to God.
To God be glory and praise for evermore.

LEADER   Everliving and generous God, all times and seasons are of your making. We commit the year ahead to your care and protection. Guide us at all times by the light of your love that we may draw closer to the gifts you have promised us. We ask this in the name of Jesus, your Son, who lives and reigns with you and the Holy Spirit, one God for ever and ever. Amen.

BLESSING

May the sun bring you new strength by day;
may the moon softly restore you by night.
may the rain wash away your fears
and the breeze invigorate your being.
May you, all the days of your life,
walk gently through the world
and know its beauty.
And may your days be good and long upon the earth.

Native American Prayer

ST VALENTINE

Scripture texts and music suggestions can be found in the Appendix

CELEBRATING RELATIONSHIPS

St Valentine's day, 14th February, is the day when we celebrate our relationships. It has in recent years become a secular/hallmark feast. It is worth celebrating as a Christian feast to remind our students that all love is a reflection of God's love for us.

By tradition, St Valentine was a bishop in the early church. There was a prohibition on all marriages except those recognised by the state. It is said that he performed Christian marriages for young couples in love. In defiance of the imperial law he was jailed and martyred. While in jail, he is believed to have cured the jailer's daughter of blindness. Just before he died he wrote her a letter which he signed 'Your Valentine'. Because of this he has become the patron saint of love

GREETING AND INTRODUCTION

OPENING PRAYER

God of love, you give us St Valentine as an example of love. His love for you was so great that he gave up his life. As we gather to celebrate the feast of this loving and caring saint we ask you to bless our relationships. May the love and affection we share for each other always be respectful and honest. May we always follow the example of your Son Jesus Christ who is Lord forever and ever. Amen.

READING

1 John 4:7-12
Love comes from God.

PSALM

Psalm: 90:12, 14, 16-17
Response: Fill us with your love, O Lord.

GOSPEL

John 3:16–17
God so loved the world that he gave his only Son.

REFLECTION

STUDENT 1   Father, you have loved us from eternity without conditions. Whether we are beautiful or plain, rich or poor, saintly or sinful, makes no different to you.

STUDENT 2   Why can't we be that way toward each other?

STUDENT 3   Why do we magnify each others shortcomings and ignore the good features?

STUDENT 4   Help us grow in love, a love that doesn't gloss over feelings, but one that accepts them.

STUDENT 5   Help us to stress what is good in all that we meet, what can be built on to help the other person become fully themselves.

STUDENT 6   Then Lord, as we increase our ability to love as Jesus did, we will come closer to the kingdom he preached. Amen

BLESSING OF VALENTINE CARDS AND GIFTS

Generous and loving God, you love us as only a parent can, without conditions, without limits. You teach us right from wrong and you fill us with your grace and love. Bless our cards and gifts which are signs of our love for one another. In the spirit of your holy bishop St Valentine, may these greeting cards and gifts bring joy and happiness to those who give and receive them. We ask this through Christ our Lord. Amen.

Cards and gifts can be sprinkled with Holy Water.

CLOSING PRAYER

Source of love and life, we keep the feast of your bishop Valentine, the patron of love. We ask you to bless our relationships with your care. Remind us that the essence of life is love and the essence of love is service. Help us to grow in love and knowledge of each other. We ask this through Christ our Lord. Amen.

ASH WEDNESDAY
BLESSING AND DISTRIBUTION
OF ASHES

Scripture texts and music suggestions can be found in the Appendix

GREETING

OPENING PRAYER

As we begin our Lenten journey we turn in prayer to our Father in heaven who will guide us on our way.

Father in heaven, you guide and direct us on our journey through life. Be with us in a special way as we begin this Lenten season of repentance. Give us the blessing of your forgiveness so that we may recall the death and resurrection of Jesus your Son with pure hearts, filled with love and respect for all he has done for us. Grant this through Christ our Lord. Amen.

READING

> Joel 2:12-18
> *(This could be dramatised by having two students with scrolls 'proclaim' the fast, alternating every few verses – a trumpet fanfare, live or recorded, might help 'Blow the Trumpet of Zion')*

PREPARING FOR THE JOURNEY

A backpack/rucksack is placed in the centre of the group. A number of students pack the items that will help us on our spiritual journey.

STUDENT 1   As we embark on our Lenten journey we pack a BIBLE and a LIST OF LENTEN RESOLUTIONS. These are the maps that will help us on our way.

STUDENT 2   As we embark on our Lenten journey we pack a BOTTLE OF WATER since this is a season when many will be preparing for baptism. Some of our journey will lead us through a desert, a place of struggle. As we thirst for God may we always rely on the spirit we received at baptism which we share with all who are baptised.

STUDENT 3   As we embark on our Lenten journey we pack a CROSS. It is our compass which points in all four directions. The vertical reminds us of our relationship with God while the horizontal calls on us to draw closer to the people around us.

STUDENT 4   As we embark on our Lenten journey we pack a CHANGE OF CLOTHES. Lent is a time of transformation when we cast off the sinfulness of our lives and put on the attitudes of goodness and love.

STUDENT 5   As we embark on our Lenten journey we pack AN ITINERARY OF PRAYER, FASTING AND ALMSGIVING which will be a constant reminder of the conversion that is needed to help us complete our trip and ensure that we have travelled closer to God and not remained still.

READING

Psalm 51
Have mercy on us, O God, in your goodness.

BLESSING OF THE ASHES

Dear friends in Christ, let us ask our Father to bless these ashes which will be used as a mark of our repentance.

Lord, bless the sinner who asks for your forgiveness and bless all those who receive these ashes. May they keep this Lenten season in preparation for the joy of Easter. We ask this through Christ our Lord. Amen.

DISTRIBUTION OF THE ASHES

The minister/leader places the ashes on those who came forward saying:

> Turn away from sin and be faithful to the Gospel
>
> *or*
>
> Remember you are dust, and to dust you will return.

Book of Blessings, p. 458

INTERCESSIONS

LEADER	As we begin our Lenten journey, we pray for God's mercy and forgiveness.
1	That the leaders of the Church will show us the way to repentance and reconciliation by their example. Lord hear us.
2	That the leaders of the nations of the world will turn away from aggression and war and do all in their power to preserve peace. Lord hear us.
3	That our acts of self-denial during this Lenten season will help us to unite with the sick, suffering and grieving members of the Church. Lord hear us.

4	That the staff and students in our school will grow in love and concern for those in need in our local communities. Lord hear us.
LEADER	Merciful Father, your son has called us to turn away from sin and return to you. Grant us the grace of your spirit to use this Lenten season to draw closer to you by our prayer, fasting and sacrifice. We ask this through Christ our Lord. Amen.
LEADER	Let us ask God our Father to forgive us our sins and to bring us to forgive those who sin against us...
	Our Father

CLOSING PRAYER

God our Father, our source of life, you know our weakness. May we reach out with joy to grasp your hand and walk more readily in your ways. We ask this through Christ our Lord.

PENITENTIAL SERVICE – LENTEN SEASON

Scripture texts and music suggestions can be found in the Appendix

HEARTS OF STONE – HEARTS OF FLESH

INTRODUCTION

LEADER   During this season of Lent, we gather to remember how much God loves us and all that he has done for us. We are all making the journey to the celebration of Easter. In this service we commit ourselves ever more completely to the path of reconciliation. We pray that the prayers we say and the sacrifices we make in this lenten season will open our hearts to receive God's forgiveness and turn our hearts of stone into hearts of flesh, places where love, honesty and justice can live.

OPENING PRAYER

Let us pray to receive the light of God's forgiveness (pause). Lord our God, our hearts seek out the warmth of your love, our minds seek out the light of your word and our souls long for your forgiveness. Give all of us the ability to grow in love so that your light may shine within us. We ask this through Christ our Lord. Amen.

READING

Isaiah 9:2-4, 6
The yoke of burden, the rod of the oppressor are smashed.

STONE RITUAL

LEADER   A basket of small stones is being passed among you. I invite you to take one each. It will represent the burdens that you carry in life. All of us, without exception, carry with us the burdens that we have gathered throughout life. We all desire to let go of these burdens, to set them down but sometimes we feel powerless to let go. Today we are going to try and get rid of the burdens that weigh us down. We will humbly approach Jesus in the sacrament of reconciliation and ask him to take our burdens away. Holding the stone in your hand, contemplate the burden it represents and ask Jesus to take it away giving you freedom.

READER 1   Lord give us the courage to change the things that we can change. Give us the serenity to accept the things we cannot change and give us the wisdom to know the difference. Help us to live one day at a time, accepting the struggles of life as the pathway to peace. In our sinfulness we turn to Jesus Christ trusting that he will make all things right if we surrender to his will.

READER 2   Jesus was the greatest healer ever known. As he walked the Holy Land people who were sick or hurting were brought to him. He laid hands on them and took away their burdens. We can ask Jesus to be our healer and to lift the burdens that weigh us down – the sins we have committed and the sins we have suffered from. May the healing touch of Jesus turn our hearts of stone into hearts of flesh.

INDIVIDUAL CONFESSION

As students make individual confession – the focus can be on their burdens – when they receive penance and absolution they can hand the stone to the priest or set it down in a particular place.

PRAYER OF HEALING

Lord Jesus, through the power of your Spirit, go back into our memories. Every hurt that has been done to us, heal the hurt. Every hurt that we have caused to other people, heal those hurts. Any relationships we have damaged or betrayed, heal those relationships. And Lord, if there is anything we can do to further reconciliation give us the grace to do so. We wish to forgive and we ask to be forgiven. Remove any bitterness that is in our hearts and fill the empty dark spaces with your love for you are the lord of life who lives and reigns for ever and ever.

Our Father...

EXCHANGE OF PEACE

CONCLUDING PRAYER

Lord, show us in these Lenten days the signs of your presence in the bits and pieces of our ordinary lives. Guide us to perform simple acts of prayer and love and sacrifice so that we may be renewed by your Holy Spirit and be ready to celebrate your resurrection. We ask this through Christ our Lord. Amen.

WAY OF THE CROSS

Scripture texts and music suggestions can be found in the Appendix

This may be suitable for use during the season of Lent. It may be an opportunity to visit a local church (if time allows). The liturgy should involve some movement, some sense of journey. Depending on time constraints the leader may choose to use some or all of the stations.

LEADER   We are here today to follow in the footsteps of Jesus. He loved us so much that he was prepared to suffer and die for us. We are grateful and want to follow his example of love. We will travel with Jesus on his final journey and learn the lessons that he teaches us by his example.

FIRST STATION
JESUS IS CONDEMNED TO DEATH

READER 1   Jesus, what happened to you was unfair and unjust. You did not deserve to be condemned but you were. The crowd shouted out to crucify you and Pilate did not have the courage to stand up for you, even though he knew you were innocent.

READER 2   Help us to be fair in our dealings with others. May we give all people the justice they deserve. Give us the courage to stand up for those who are treated unfairly even if it means going against popular opinion.

Second Station

JESUS RECEIVES HIS CROSS

READER 1   Jesus, the burden that was placed upon your shoulders was very heavy. You took upon yourself the pain and suffering of others.

READER 2   Help us Jesus when we are in trouble or difficulty. May we have the strength to get through our times of need. Give us the faith to believe you are with us when we need you most.

Third Station

JESUS FALLS THE FIRST TIME

READER 1   Jesus, the road was rough and the cross was heavy. You stumbled under its weight and fell to the ground.

READER 2   Help us Jesus when we make mistakes in our lives. May we have the wisdom to learn from the mistakes we make. Give us the hope to continue on our Christian lives.

Fourth Station

JESUS MEETS HIS MOTHER

READER 1   Jesus, you met your mother after you had been condemned as a criminal. Your love for each other gave you both the support you needed in this difficult time.

READER 2   Help us Jesus to remember that our parents love us, even when we fight. May we always respect them. Give us the grace to respond to them always in love.

Fifth Station
Simon of Cyrene helps Jesus to carry his cross

READER 1   Jesus, in your great need you received help from a stranger – someone who didn't even know you.

READER 2   Help us Jesus, to see the needs of people everywhere. May we have the vision to see the suffering Jesus in people everywhere. Give us the generosity to respond in love to the needs of people we may not even know.

Sixth Station
Veronica wipes the face of Jesus

READER 1   Jesus, the crowd around you was angry and abusive. One woman had the courage to step out from the crowd. For Veronica love was stronger than fear.

READER 2   Help us Jesus to act properly in difficult situations. May we have the courage of our convictions. Give us the strength to stand out from the crowd and do what is right.

Seventh Station
Jesus falls the second time

READER 1   Jesus, you were the son of God but you were human too. The burden of the cross became heavier with each passing step until you could go no further and you fell again.

READER 2   Help us Jesus when we feel overwhelmed by trouble or difficulties. May we have the ability to carry on with your example. Give us the strength we need in moments of weakness.

Eighth Station
Jesus consoles the women of Jerusalem

READER 1   Jesus, even in the painful journey your first concern was the comfort and consolation of others. In your own pain you took time to say words of healing to others who suffered.

READER 2   Help us Jesus to recognise the pain and suffering of other people. May we never be so wrapped up in ourselves that we ignore those around us. Give us the openness to see the needs of all.

Ninth Station
Jesus falls the third time

READER 1   Jesus, we are surprised that you are on the ground for the third time. Can you really be so frail, so weak in your humanity?

READER 2   Help us Jesus to be tolerant of human frailty. May we always treat those who fail with dignity and respect. Give us the vision to see Jesus in all people, even in those who let us down.

Tenth Station
Jesus is stripped of his garments

READER 1   Jesus, even in these last moments of your life you are being denied your human dignity. The soldiers strip you of your clothing, leaving you naked and vulnerable.

READER 2   Help us Jesus, in the times when we are weak and vulnerable. May we always respect the dignity of every human person. Give us the ability to see the dignity of people, no matter what their circumstances.

ELEVENTH STATION
JESUS IS NAILED TO THE CROSS

READER 1   Jesus, the manner of your death is cruel and inhuman. Having carried your cross through the jeering mob you are made to suffer even greater torture before you die.

Reader 2   Help us Jesus to support the victims of torture in our modern world. May we work to promote awareness of suffering and injustice. Give society the sense of justice it needs to change itself.

TWELFTH STATION
JESUS DIES ON THE CROSS

READER 1   Jesus, your death left those you love in great pain and grief. They were confused and afraid. They felt lonely and isolated.

READER 2   Help us, Jesus, in our moments of grief and suffering. May we comforted by the memories of the good times we have shared with those we love. Give us the precious gifts of consolation and comfort in our times of loss.

THIRTEENTH STATION
JESUS IS TAKEN DOWN FROM THE CROSS

READER 1   Jesus, this must have been a moment of terrible grief for your mother as she cradled your lifeless body in her arms. There was probably a sense of hopelessness and despair among those who believed and hoped in you.

READER 2   Help us, Jesus, in the moments of our lives where it seems like there is no hope or solution. May we always be able to cope with disappointment in our lives. Give us the confidence that after the darkness there is always sunrise.

FOURTEENTH STATION
JESUS IS LAID IN THE TOMB

READER 1   Jesus, even the grave you occupied in death was not your own, but borrowed from a follower. As the stone was rolled across did your followers see their hopes and dreams entombed with your body?

READER 2   Help us, Jesus, to see that there is life and love beyond the grave. May we always have confidence in the promise of eternal life that you have made. Give us that gift of life with you and all those we love and care for.

CONCLUSION

Distribute 'Cross in my Pocket' and prayer card.

Cross in My Pocket

I carry a cross in my pocket
A simple reminder to me
Of the fact that I am a Christian
No matter where I may be.

This little cross is not magic
Nor is it a good luck charm.
It isn't meant to protect me.
From every physical harm.

It's not for identification
For all the world to see.
It's simply an understanding
Between my Saviour and me.

When I put my hand in my pocket
To bring out a coin or key.
The cross is there to remind me
Of the price he paid for me.

It reminds me, too, to be thankful
For my blessings day by day
And strive to serve him better
In all that I do and say.

It's also a daily reminder
Of the peace and comfort I share
With all who know my master
And give themselves to his care.

So, I carry a cross in my pocket
Reminding no one but me
That Jesus Christ is Lord of my life
If only I'll let him be.

Verna Thomas

SERVICE OF HEALING

Scripture texts and music suggestions can be found in the Appendix

PRAYER FOR SOMEONE WHO IS ILL

Not for use every time a child is absent but perhaps when a child is more seriously ill or awaiting surgery – a time when there may be a need to reassure students and give them confidence. We can begin by inviting students to fill in get-well cards or expressions of hope for a speedy recovery. If possible, place a picture of the sick person in a central location with a candle beside it. Place some lighted charcoal in a saucer before picture.

GREETING

LEADER   God of compassion, we gather today to pray for _____, our classmate who is ill. As we light this candle, may its flame remind us of our love that burns always in our hearts, whether we are healthy or sick. May it also remind us of the light you bring into our lives, and the warmth of your tender embrace.

                Light candle beside photo.

READING

                James 5:13-16
                The prayer of faith will save the one who is ill.

PSALM

                Psalm 25:4-5, 8-9, 10, 14, 15-16
                Response: To you, O Lord, I lift up my soul.

Cure of Peter's mother-in-law.
Matthew 8:14-17
Christ bore our sicknesses.

PRAYERS OF INTERCESSION

God is with us always and in the same way we know God is with _____, who is sick. With this trust let us bring our petitions to God. As we pray, we light this incense, the pleasing fragrance that rises before God like our spirits and our needs.

Put some incense on charcoal before picture.

READER	Our response is 'Lord, hear our prayer'.
1	For _____ in this time of sickness, we pray to the Lord.
2	For _____'s family as they take care of him, we pray to the Lord.
3	For all of us who miss _____ and pray for a full recovery, we pray to the Lord.
4	For all those who are sick and the people who care for them, we pray to the Lord.
LEADER	Lord Jesus Christ, you care for each of us as tenderly as a mother cares for her child. You gather us in your arms and gently carry us when we are weak. We commend to your loving care our classmate _____. We ask that he/she will be healed in whatever way possible. Help him/her to know the comforting presence of your Spirit, that he/she may soon join us again at school. We ask this through Christ our Lord.

I invite you now to hold us the cards or greetings you have put together for _____ so we can ask God to bless them.

Loving God, these cards and greetings are an expression of our care and concern for _____. Bless them with your healing love and when they are given to _____ they will bring the peace and warmth of your spirit. We ask this through Christ our Lord. Amen.

Our Father ....

Sign of the Cross.

THE WAILING WALL

Scripture texts and music suggestions can be found in the Appendix

GATHERING THE PRAYERS OF AN ENTIRE SCHOOL COMMUNITY

This may be more suitable for a school with its own oratory or prayer room. On one wall put up a notice board that has been painted to simulate brick wall. Somewhere near put up a note of explanation.

This is an idea inspired by the Wailing Wall in Jerusalem. The Wailing Wall is the Western wall of the Old Temple. At this spot many generations of people have offered their prayers to God for all their needs. Even today people write down their petitions and prayers and place them in the cracks between the brick. Our wall here serves the same purpose. You can:

1. Tack up your needs, and prayers so that all who see it may be moved to pray.

2. You might consider taking a petition from the wall, keeping it for a few days while praying for the unknown writer. Then you might initial it and put it back so that the person whose heart is broken will know that there is someone who gives comfort and is concerned.

This is a place where we can raise our minds and hearts to God. Let us pray, in reverence for our own needs and in charity for the needs of others.

Pens and pieces of paper should be available for use. When it has been there a while we can celebrate a liturgy for all the needs and celebrate the power of prayer.

GREETING

OPENING PRAYER

God our Creator, you have given us the many gifts we need to live our lives well. Help us always to be mindful of the needs of people around us. Give us the grace to be able to turn to you in our own times of need. Teach us the words to use when we pray. We ask this through our Lord Jesus Christ, who lives and reigns with you and the Holy Spirit, one God forever and ever. Amen.

LITURGY OF THE WORD
Power of Prayer

READING

> 1 Timothy 2:1-4
> *Let prayers be offered for everyone to God.*

PSALM

> Psalm 25:1-2 and 4, 5, 6
> *Response:* To you, O Lord, I lift up my soul.

GOSPEL

> Matthew 6:7-13
> *This is how you should pray.*

The prayers of petition are gathered from the wailing wall and brought to the centre of the assembly where a fire has been prepared (methylated spirits). The leader of the liturgy may choose to read some of them aloud (these should perhaps be chosen in advance). He/she then takes them and places them in the fire bucket.

God our Father of love, bless these requests which have hung on our wailing wall. These are cries from the heart and we ask you to hear them and to listen to our own needs as well. As we touch them to the fire and they wind their way to heaven before the throne of your mercy, have pity on those who wrote them. Listen to all our cries, for you have made us and we are your own. Lord have mercy on us as we make our plea through Christ Our Lord. Amen.

INTRODUCTION TO OUR FATHER

LEADER   God of love, you have taught us to pray to you for all our needs whether physical or spiritual. Inspired by confidence in your promises we turn to you as a family united in prayer to say the words your son has taught us.

Our Father ...

CONCLUDING PRAYER

Generous and loving God, you know the needs of your children before we even ask. Please listen to us as we turn to you in prayer, not only for ourselves but also for those who find it difficult to do so. Give us all the words to speak to you and help us to grow closer to you and to one another. We ask this through Christ our Lord. Amen.

BLESSING

May God the Father bless us with every good gift. May God's only Son Jesus Christ strengthen us in love for one another and may God's Holy Spirit give us the courage to always turn to Him in our need. Amen.

A LITURGY FOR EXAMINATIONS

Scripture texts and music suggestions can be found in the Appendix

This is a short liturgy, 10 to 15 minutes, and can be used on the morning of exams or at the beginning of public exams – it might be a good way to settle nerves and focus students. It would be nice to have a gift for students to take away to their exams – a prayer card, a cross, a dove, a pin. It will be a reminder of some peace and relaxation in the exam hall.

GREETING AND INTRODUCTION

Welcome students, put them at their ease – try to give them some peace in their anxiety.

OPENING PRAYER

Loving God, we come before you on this day when we begin our exams. We are anxious and a little nervous. There is fear in our lives and we seek your perfect love which casts out all fear. Give us Lord, the vision to see the path you set before us, give us the gift of recall as we are tested today so that we may do our best with the talents you have given us. We ask this through Christ our Lord.

Ecclesiastes 11:7-10
Banish anxiety from your mind.

PRAYER TO THE HOLY SPIRIT

Come Holy Spirit, Divine Creator
true source of light and fountain of all wisdom.
Pour out your brilliance upon my intellect,
send away any anxiety and worry that surrounds me on this my examination day.
Give to me,
a penetrating mind to understand,
a retentive memory,
method and ease in learning,
the clarity to comprehend, and
abundant grace in expressing myself.
Guide the beginning of my work,
direct its progress
and bring it to successful completion

adapted from Thomas Aquinas

INTERCESSIONS

LEADER   Heavenly Father, we gather in prayer on this examination day to ask your blessing on these students. Give them the gifts and graces they need to sustain them today and in the days ahead.

1   For all students who start exams today, that God's spirit may give them the gift of wisdom and understanding. Lord hear us.

2	For all those who are nervous or afraid, that they may know the peace of God in their moments of need. Lord hear us.
3	For all those who have worked to prepare us for these days of testing, that they may have the reward of their goodness to us. Lord hear us.
4	For our parents and families who support us in all that we do, give them the confidence of knowing they have done their best for us. Lord hear us.
5	For those who will supervise and correct our exams, that they may always be fair and just. Lord hear us.
LEADER	Lord our God, send your spirit upon these students and fill them with your wisdom and blessings. Give them your perfect love which casts out all fear. We ask this in the name of Jesus the Lord. Amen.

Our Father

EXCHANGE OF PEACE

CONCLUDING PRAYER

Dear Lord
Teach me to live my life.
Teach me to know how to use all the good I have inside of me.
Teach me to think right, speak good words, and do good deeds.
Teach me to see the good in all.
Teach me to share with my fellow human beings in respect and love.
Teach me love.
We ask this through Christ our Lord. Amen.

TEST PRAYER FOR SUFFERING STUDENTS

Something that might give a little laugh and relieve tension.

Now that I lay me down to study,
I pray the Lord I won't go nutty.
If I should fail to learn this junk,
I pray the Lord I will not flunk.

But if I do, don't pity me at all;
Just lay my bones down in study hall.
Tell my teachers I did my best.
Then pile the books upon my chest.

Now I lay me down to rest,
And pray I'll pass tomorrow's test.
If I should die before I wake,
That's one less test I'll have to take.

Amen!

A LITURGY TO MARK THE END OF THE SCHOOL YEAR

Scripture texts and music suggestions can be found in the Appendix

INTRODUCTION

Welcome to our liturgy to mark the end of another school year. It is a time of joy and sadness, of eagerness and reluctance. We celebrate the unity we have shared in this past year and we ask God's blessing on all students who will soon begin their holidays.

GREETING

OPENING PRAYER

Loving God, you created our world and filled it with wonderful gifts. You sent your son, Jesus, to live in us and among us, telling us of your deep and lasting love. We love you, Jesus, and want to walk in the brightness of your love. Send your spirit to be with us and open us to your peace, love and joy. We ask this through Christ our Lord. Amen.

PENITENTIAL RITE

We ask God's forgiveness for the times we have been unkind to others, for the ways in which we have forgotten God, been ungrateful to him or to others.

Lord, you have come to call sinners to yourself.
Lord have mercy.

Lord, you forgave all who hurt you.
Christ have mercy.

Lord, you have opened for us the gates of heaven.
Lord have mercy.

READING

Phillipians 4:4-9
Rejoice in the Lord

PSALM

Psalm 150:1-2, 3-4, 5-6
Response: Let everything that lives give praise to God.

GOSPEL

John 15:12-17
Love one another as I have loved you.

INTERCESSIONS

LEADER	As we prepare to go our separate ways during this holiday season we turn to God who unites us even when we are apart. He listens to our prayers and provides for our needs.
READER	Our response is: *Lord hear our prayer.*
1	May the Holy Spirit guide us as we continue to develop our relationship with God. *We pray to the Lord.*
2	May we always turn to God to seek help with the difficulties and decisions we will meet in our time apart. *We pray to the Lord.*

| 3 | May we always remember how unique and important each one of us is and that we are responsible for ourselves and the consequences of our actions. |

We pray to the Lord.

| 4 | We thank God for our friends, may we always realise the importance of being a good friend and the good support that friends give. |

We pray to the Lord.

| 5 | For our parents and families, for their patience, support and love. |

We pray to the Lord.

| 6 | For our teachers and all in the school who have helped us grow, develop and learn. |

We pray to the Lord.

| LEADER | God in heaven, you know our needs even before we turn to you. Listen to our prayers for each other as this school year draws to a close. Watch over us all and keep us safe until we are united again in your love. We ask this through Christ our Lord. |

RITE OF LEAVETAKING

In advance of the liturgy some coloured card/paper can be cut to business-card size and distributed to the class; each member can write their name and address on a card. These are then placed in a basket and during the liturgy students can draw out a card. They will commit to pray for that student and maybe send them a postcard during the holidays.

Reader   Our lives are marked forever by those we meet; the friendships we make and the love we experience, the quarrels and the reconciliations, the work we have tried to do together for each other and for those less fortunate. All this has given us something that will last. Long after we have forgotten marks and results, we will remember the friendships, the times of growth. We will remember how we helped each other grow in faith, hope and in love. May what we have learned and shared here give us help in our lives.

REFLECTION

There's a Star inside of me;
she shines there in my heart
and waits to be recognised.

Darkness tries to scare her off,
ego attempts to ignore her,
busyness pushes her around.
But this wonderful shining Star
keeps twinkling, all aglow.

She waits to lead me
to an unknown meadow
where the truth of who I am
will be revealed to me.

Shining Star, faithful Star,
when will I follow you?
When will I come to the meadow
where the truth will set me free?

Joyce Rupp

CONCLUDING PRAYER

Creator God, we praise you for your glory and thank you for your goodness to us. Look on all of us with your love and bless us as this school year draws to a close. May the Holy Spirit strengthen our talents and skills and help us use them for your glory and for the good of all people. We ask this grace through Christ our Lord. Amen.

A GRADUATION LITURGY

Scripture texts and music suggestions can be found in the Appendix

GATHERING RITUAL

The Easter/Paschal candle is lit in a prominent place. On the altar/sacred space there are four unlit candles. A student introduces the Liturgy.

STUDENT   On behalf of all the final year students here in _____, I welcome you all who have come to share this special evening with us. Each of you have made a contribution to this stage of life's journey for us. We gather to say thanks to God for all that has been. We gather to ask God for the gifts and graces we need as we begin the next stage of life's journey.

A parent steps forward and, using a taper, lights the first candle from the Easter Candle.

PARENT   On behalf of the parents who are here this evening, I offer you the light of love. Carry this light of love out into the world. When you find the light of love is flickering, or threatened by the troubles of life, remember that there will always be a light burning for you in that place called home.

A teacher lights the second candle in the same way.

TEACHER   On behalf of the staff of the school, I offer you the light of wisdom. Carry this light of wisdom out into the world. When faced with choices and decisions that you never before dreamed of may you be inspired by wisdom to find the good and the true.

A student (junior to the graduates) lights the third candle.

STUDENT   On behalf of all the students that you leave behind, I offer you the light of memory. Carry the light of these days out into the world. Remember those of us who remain to continue the story of this school. Remember us and we will remember you.

                A trustee/member of the board lights the fourth candle.

TRUSTEE   On behalf of the trustees and management of this school, I offer you the light of faith. Carry this light of faith out into the world. Remember to be part of the Christian community wherever you find it and be a light for the world.

OPENING PRAYER

God of love and hope, you accompany each one of us on our journey through life. Give us a sense of gratitude for all that is past, a sense of joy in this present moment and a sense of courage so that we can face the future confident in your presence in our lives. We ask this through our Lord Jesus Christ, your son who lives and reigns with you and the Holy Spirit. One God, for ever and ever. Amen.

LITURGY OF THE WORD

FIRST READING

        Ecclesiastes 3:1-8
        A time for everything

PSALM

        Psalm 113:1-2, 3-4, 5-6
        Response: Blessed by the name of the Lord forever.

SECOND READING

        Philippians 4:4-7
        Be happy in the Lord

GOSPEL

Luke 24:13-39
Disciples on Road to Emmaus

SERVICE OF COMMITMENT TO CHRISTIAN LIVING

All graduates stand while the congregation remain seated.

LEADER   The light of God is the light of love,
              Love is our origin,
              Love is our constant calling,
              Love is our destiny in heaven,
              Love is the light of life,
              Jesus lost his very life in love of the cross,
              The struggle to love is one of life's greatest challenges.

              (The leader takes a light from the Easter candle and passes it among the graduates, each of whom has a night-light)

LEADER   Take this light which you first received in baptism. May it ever burn in your heart. Let it shine before all people so that you may give glory to your father in heaven.

GRADUATES   Amen

LEADER   Parents, families, teachers and friends, we are privileged to be here tonight witnessing these young people begin another stage of their journey of life. You have helped them in so many ways to reach this stage and so I ask you to continue in support and encouragement of these young people by your actions and prayers.

              We are gathered here in celebration of our time together, an ending and beginning and so I ask you:

              Are you preparing for your life ahead with commitment and enthusiasm?

GRADUATES	We are.
LEADER	Have you undertaken the responsibilities of maturing in respect, tolerance and trustworthiness?
GRADUATES	We have.
LEADER	Do you promise to accept the opportunities of life with joy and energy?
GRADUATES	We do.
LEADER	Have you the desire to grow in faith and live the gospel values in everyday life?
GRADUATES	We have.
LEADER	You are God's children, the children of God's kingdom. May each one of you grow in wisdom and strength and come to a knowledge of the God who loves you.
ALL	Amen.

PRAYERS OF INTERCESSION

1 **God of Love**

Grant that the Pope and the leaders of your Church may find constant strength and inspiration from the loving example of your Son who gave power to the powerless and dignity to those who felt worthless. Lord hear us.

2 **God of Justice**

May the example of your Son who fed the hungry and raised the dead move our minds and hearts to find ways of making our world a world of life and not of suffering and death. Lord hear us.

3   **God of Hope**

Your Son showed us that love is they key which unlocks the dark prison of hatred and prejudice. May all who live on this land learn to use this key. Lord hear us.

4   **God of Strength**

May all who are entrusted with the care of the young never lose faith in the work that they do. May they, like Jesus, find in you a constant source of energy and renewal. Lord hear us.

5   **God of Wisdom**

On the days of our exams protect us from anxiety and fear so that we will be able to do our best. Be our guide and friend now and in the future.

6   **God of Mercy**

We remember with love and affection our loved ones who sadly cannot be with us tonight. We thank you for the wonderful years and memories we shared with them. Lord hear us.

SOME PRAYERS AND REFLECTIONS FOR GRADUATION/END OF YEAR

Our deepest fear is not that we are inadequate. Our deepest fear is that we are powerful beyond measure: it is our light, not our darkness, that most frightens us. We ask ourselves, who am I to be brilliant, gorgeous, talented, fabulous? Actually, who are you not to be. You are a child of God. Your playing small doesn't serve the world. There is nothing enlightened about shrinking so that other people won't feel insecure around you. You are all meant to shine, as children do. We were born to make manifest the glory of God that is within us. It is not just in some of us; it's in everyone. And as we let our own light shine, we unconsciously give other people permission to do the same. As we're liberated from our own fear, our presence automatically liberates others.

Nelson Mandela, 1994 Inaugural Presidential Speech

REFLECTION

May you find serenity and tranquillity in a world you may not always understand
May the pain you have known and the conflict you have experienced give you the strength to walk through life facing each new situation with courage and optimism.
Always know that there are those whose love and understanding will always be there, even when you feel most alone.
May you discover enough goodness in others to believe in a world of peace.
May a kind word, a reassuring touch, a warm smile be yours every day of your life, and may you give these gifts as well as receive them.
Remember the sunshine when the storm seems unending.
Teach love to those who know hate, and let that love embrace you, so that you may call upon them.

May the teaching of those you admire become part of you, so that you may call upon them.

Remember, those whose lives you have touched and who have touched yours are always a part of you, even if the encounters were less than you would have wished.

It is the content of the encounter that is more important than its form.

May you not become too concerned with material matters, but instead place immeasurable value on the goodness in your heart.

Find time in each day to see the beauty and love in the world around you.

Realise that each person has limitless abilities, but each of us is different in our own way.

What you may feel you lack in one regard may be more than compensated for in another.

What you feel you lack in the present may become one of your strengths in the future.

May you see your future as one filled with promise and possibility.

Learn to view everything as a worthwhile experience.

May you find enough inner strength to determine your own worth by yourself, and not be dependent on another's judgements of your accomplishments.

May you always feel loved.

REFLECTIONS OF A PARENT

I gave you life,
but cannot live it for you.

I can give you directions,
but I cannot be there to lead you.

I can take you to church
but I cannot make you believe.

I can teach you right from wrong,
but I cannot always decide for you.

I can buy you beautiful clothes,
but I cannot make you beautiful inside.

I can offer you advice,
but I cannot accept it for you.

I can give you love,
but I cannot force it upon you.

I can teach you to share,
but I cannot make you unselfish.

I can teach you to respect,
but I cannot force you to show honour.

I can advise you about friends,
but I cannot choose them for you.

I can advise you about sex,
but I cannot keep you pure.

I can tell you about alcohol and drugs,
but I can't say 'No' for you.

I can tell you about lofty goals,
but I can't achieve them for you.

I can teach you about kindness,
but I can't force you to be gracious.

I can pray for you,
but I cannot make you walk with God.

I can tell you how to live,
but I cannot give you eternal life.

I can love you with unconditional love all of my life...
and I will.

APPENDIX

MUSIC

RESOURCES

(CHE 1) *Celebration Hymnal for Everyone Volume 1,* edited by Patrick Geary
(McCrimmons, ISBN: 0 85597 536 9A)

(CHE 2) *Celebration Hymnal for Everyone Volume 2,* edited by Patrick Geary
(McCrimmons, ISBN: 0 85597 536 9A)

(IC) I*n Caelo – songs for a pilgrim people,* edited by Liam Lawton
(Veritas, ISBN: 1 85390 466X)

(MC) *Michael Card – Joy in the Journey*
Available from www.michaelcard.com

CHECKLIST

1.   Once music has been chosen:

        a.   Check the key of the piece, especially if students are being asked to sing along with a CD. The atmosphere can be ruined by a piece being sung too low or too high.

        b.   Not all verses are necessarily suitable to the liturgy at hand. Select the verses carefully beforehand.

        c.   Make sure copies of the words are available for everyone.

2.   The use of instrumental music can be very powerful during liturgies – there is a huge amount of suitable traditional music available, especially many beautiful slow airs that fit well with reconciliation services, offertory processions, Easter liturgies, and so on. Even a solo tin whistle works well in this context.

3.   The use of classical music should not be avoided, especially if music students are present. A piece with a definite melody usually works best. Try using some CDs featuring instrumental solos, for example, David Agnew's *Into the Mist*, which features solo oboe.

4.   If you find Taizé chants are favourably received, try some Gregorian chant.

MUSIC SUGGESTIONS TO ACCOMPANY LITURGIES

1.   **MASS FOR THE BEGINNING OF THE SCHOOL YEAR**
        Gather, Liam Lawton (GIA Publications)
        O that today you would listen, Chris O'Hara (CHE 2)
        Who calls you by name, David Haas (CHE 1)
        This is my body, Jimmy Owens (CHE 2)
        Gifts of bread and wine, Christine McCann (CHE 2)
        Song of the body of Christ, David Haas (CHE 2)
        Eat this bread, Taizé
        Now in this banquet, Marty Haugen (CHE 2)
        We come to your feast, Michael Joncas (IC)
        Come to the table, Michael Card (MC)

2.   **CHARITY**
        God has chosen me, Bernadette Farrell (CHE 1)
        Blessed are they the poor in spirit, David Haas (CHE 1)
        Let every human heart, Liam Lawton (GIA Publications)
        Ubi caritas, Taizé
        Whatsoever you do, Willard F. Jabusch (CHE 2)
        Here am I Lord, T. Valentine (GIA Publications)

3.   **CELEBRATION OF CREATION**
        Glory and praise to our God, Daniel L. Schutte (CHE 1)
        Alleluia, this is the day, Marty Haugen (CHE 1)
        All the ends of the earth, Marty Haugen & David Haas (CHE 1)

Come, let us sing for joy, Marty Haugen (GIA Publications)
Sing a new song to the Lord, David Wilson (CHE 2)
Sing to the mountains, Bob Dufford SJ (CHE 2)
African glory to God, Kirner/Warner (World Library Publications)

4.   **COMMEMORATION OF THE FAITHFUL DEPARTED**
The clouds' veil, Liam Lawton (IC)
We give you thanks, David Haas (Gia Publications)
On eagle's wings, Michael Joncas (CHE 2)
I am the bread of life, Suzanne Toolan (CHE 1)
Be still and know that I am with you, Anne Scott (CHE 1)
The Lord is my Shepherd, Bernard Sexton (Maynooth Summer School 2002)

5.   **CELEBRATION OF ADVENT**
Emmanuel, Michael Card (MC)
The maiden and her child, Liam Lawton (GIA Publications)
Wait for the Lord, Jacques Berthier (CHE 2)
Long ago prophets knew, Piae Cantions (Stainer & Bell Ltd)

6.   **SERVICE OF RECONCILIATION**
Bless the Lord my soul, Taizé
All I once held dear, Graham Kendrick (IC)
Emmanuel, Michael Card (MC)
City of God, Daniel L. Schutte (CHE 1)
The servant king, Graham Kendrick (CHE 1)
The summons, Bell & Maule (CHE 2)
I will be with you, Gerald Markland (CHE 1)

7.   **A CELEBRATION FOR THE NEW YEAR**
Who calls you by name, David Haas (CHE 1)
All you works of God, Marty Haugen (GIA Publications)
Laudate omnes gentes, Taizé (IC)
Christ be our light, Bernadette Farrell (IC)
Canticle of the sun, Marty Haugen (IC)

8. **ST VALENTINE**

I will be the vine, Liam Lawton (IC)

The final word, Michael Card (MC)

Sing a Song to the Lord, Liam Lawton (GIA Publications)

9. **ASH WEDNESDAY – BLESSING AND DISTRIBUTION OF ASHES**

Be still and know I am with you, Anne Scott (CHE 1)

Bless the Lord my soul, Jacques Berthier (CHE 1)

Wait for the Lord, Taizé

40 days and 40 nights, M. Herbst (CHE 1)

Wait for the Lord, Jacques Berthier (CHE 2)

Turn to me, John B. Foley SJ (CHE 2)

Come back to me, Gregory Norbet (CHE 1)

Be still and know that I am God, Steven Warner (World Library Publications)

10. **PENITENTIAL SERVICE – LENTEN SEASON**

Bless the Lord, Taize

Come back to me, Gregory Norbet (CHE 1)

Turn to me, John B. Foley SJ (CHE 2)

I will be the vine, Liam Lawton (IC)

You are mine, David Haas (IC)

11. **WAY OF THE CROSS**

Out of darkness, Tom Kendzia (IC)

O comfort my people, C. Waddell OSCO (IC)

Ours were the sufferings, Francesca Leftley (CHE 2)

Jesus, remember me, Taizé

Keep watch with me, Margaret Rizza (Kevin Mayhew Ltd)

12. **SERVICE OF HEALING**

Be still and know I am with you, Anne Scott (CHE 1)

You are mine, David Haas (IC)

I will never forget you, Carey Landry (CHE 1)

Lay your hands, Carey Landry (CHE 1)

Be still and know that I am God, Anon. (CHE 1)

13.   **THE WAILING WALL**

The cry of the poor, John B. Foley SJ (CHE 2)

That's what faith must be, Michael Card (CHE 2)

Be with me, Lord, Michael Joncas (CHE 1)

You are mine, David Haas (IC)

14.   **A LITURGY FOR EXAMINATIONS**

Lord of all hopefulness*, Jan Struther (IC)

Be still and know that I am God, Anon. (CHE 1)

Shepherd song, Bernard Sexton (Maynooth Summer School 2002)

Blessed be the Lord, Daniel L. Schutte (CHE 1)

O Lord hear my prayer, Jacques Berthier (CHE 2)

In our need, Patrick Geary (CHE 1)

Bí Íosa Im Chroise, traditional Irish melody (IC)

*   *To accompany 'Test Prayer for Suffering Students'!*

15.   **A LITURGY TO MARK THE END OF THE SCHOOL YEAR**

You are mine, David Haas (IC)

Joy in the journey, Michael Card (MC)

I will follow Him, from Sister Act 1

Siahamba, traditional Bantu melody (CHE 2)

This is my will, Stephen Deane (CHE 2)

Covenant Hymn, Rory Cooney (GIA Publications)

Though the mountains may fall, David L. Schutte (CHE 2)

A new commandment I give unto you, Anon. (CHE 1)

16.   **A GRADUATION LITURGY**

Where your treasure is, Marty Haugen (GIA Publications)

I will be with you, Gerald Markland (CHE 1)

Set your hearts on the higher gifts, Steven Warner
        (World Library Publications)

Sing of the Lord's Goodness, Ernest Sands (CHE 2)

How can I keep from singing, Steven Warner (World Library Publications)

May God bless and keep you, Christopher Walker (CHE 1)

SCRIPTURE READINGS

1   **MASS FOR THE BEGINNING OF THE SCHOOL YEAR**

Ecclesiastes 11-12

Send out your bread upon the waters, for after many days you will get it back. Divide your means seven ways, or even eight, for you do not know what disaster may happen on earth. When clouds are full, they empty rain on the earth; whether a tree falls to the south or to the north, in the place where the tree falls, there it will lie. Whoever observes the wind will not sow; and whoever regards the clouds will not reap. Just as you do not know how the breath comes to the bones in the mother's womb, so you do not know the work of God, who makes everything. In the morning sow your seed, and at evening do not let your hands be idle; for you do not know which will prosper, this or that, or whether both alike will be good. Light is sweet, and it is pleasant for the eyes to see the sun. Even those who live many years should rejoice in them all; yet let them remember that the days of darkness will be many. All that comes is vanity. Rejoice, young man, while you are young, and let your heart cheer you in the days of your youth. Follow the inclination of your heart and the desire of your eyes, but know that for all these things God will bring into judgment. Banish anxiety from your mind, and put away pain from your body; for youth and the dawn of life are vanity.

Remember your creator in the days of your youth, before the days of trouble come, and the years draw near when you will say, 'I have no pleasure in them'; before the sun and the light and the moon and the stars are darkened and the clouds return with the rain; in the day when the guards of the house tremble, and the strong men are bent, and the women who grind cease working because they are few, and those who look through the windows see dimly; when the doors on the street are shut, and the sound of the grinding is low, and one rises up at the sound of a bird, and all the daughters of song are brought low; when one is afraid of heights, and terrors are in the road; the almond tree blossoms, the grasshopper drags itself along and desire fails; because all must go to their eternal home, and the mourners will go about the streets; before the silver cord is snapped, and the golden bowl is broken, and the pitcher is broken at the fountain, and the wheel broken at the cistern, and the dust returns to the earth as it was, and the breath returns to God who gave it. Vanity of vanities, says the Teacher, all is vanity. Besides being wise, the Teacher also taught the people knowledge, weighing and studying and arranging many proverbs. The Teacher sought to find pleasing words, and he wrote words of truth plainly.

The sayings of the wise are like goads, and like nails firmly fixed are the collected sayings that are given by one shepherd. Of anything beyond these, my child, beware. Of making many books there is no end, and much study is a weariness of the flesh The end of the matter; all has been heard. Fear God, and keep his commandments; for that is the whole duty of everyone. For God will bring every deed into judgment, including every secret thing, whether good or evil.

Psalm 95: 1-2; 3-5

O come, let us to sing to the Lord; let us make a joyful noise to the rock of our salvation!

Let us come into his presence with thanksgiving; let us make a joyful noise to him with songs of praise!

For the Lord is a great God, and a great king above all gods.

In his hand are the depths of the earth; the heights of the mountains are his also.

The sea is his, for he made it, and the dry land, which his hands have formed.

Matthew 13:44-46

The kingdom of heaven is like treasure hidden in a field, which someone found and hid; then in his joy he goes and sells all that he has and buys that field.

Again, the kingdom of heaven is like a merchant in search of fine pearls; on finding one pearl of great value, he went and sold all that he had and bought it.

2. **CHARITY**

2 Corinthians 8:1-3, 12

We want you to know, brothers and sisters, about the grace of God that has been granted to the churches of Macedonia; for during a severe ordeal of affliction, their abundant joy and their extreme poverty have overflowed in a wealth of generosity on their part. For, as I can testify, they voluntarily gave according to their means...

For if the eagerness is there, the gift is acceptable according to what one has – not according to what one does not have.

Psalm 103:1, 2, 5, 11

Bless the Lord, O my soul,
and all that is within me,
bless his holy name.

Bless the Lord, O my soul
and do not forget all his benefits ...

who satisfies you with good as
long as you live
so that your youth is renewed
like the eagle's.

For as the heavens are high
above the earth
so great is his steadfast love
toward those who fear him;

Matthew 6:1-4

Beware of practicing your piety before others in order to be seen by them; for then you have no reward from your Father in heaven.

So whenever you give alms, do not sound a trumpet before you, as the hypocrites do in the synagogues and in the streets, so that they may be praised by others. Truly I tell you, they have received their reward. But when you give alms, do not let your left hand know what you right hand is doing, so that your aims may be done in secret; and your Father who sees in secret will reward you.

3.   **CELEBRATION OF CREATION**

Deuteronomy 8:7-10

For the Lord your God is bringing you into a good land, a land with flowing streams, with springs and underground waters welling up in valleys and hills, a land of wheat and barley, of vines and fig trees and pomegranates, a land of olive trees and honey, a land where you may eat bread without scarcity, where you will lack nothing, a land whose stones are iron and from whose hills you may mine copper.

You shall eat your fill and bless the Lord your God for the good land that he has taken you.

Psalm 147:5, 7, 8

Great is our Lord, and abundant in power;
his understanding is beyond measure.

Sing to the Lord with thanksgiving;
make melody to our God on the lyre.
He covers the heavens with clouds,
prepares rain for the earth,
makes grass grow on the hills.

Luke 12:15-21

And he said to them, 'Take care! Be on your guard against all kinds of greed; for one's life does not consist in the abundance of possessions.' Then he told them a parable: 'The land of a rich man produced abundantly. And he thought to himself, "What should I do, for I have no place to store my crops?" Then he said, "I will do this: I will pull down my barns and build larger ones, and there I will store all my grain and my goods. And I will say to my soul, 'Soul you have ample goods laid up for many years; relax, eat, drink, be merry.'" But God said to him, "You fool! This very night your life is being demanded of you. And the things you have prepared, whose will they be?" So it is with those who store up treasures for themselves but are not richer toward God.'

4. COMMEMORATION OF THE FAITHFUL DEPARTED

1 John 3:1-2

Now there was a Pharisee named Nicodemus, a leader of the Jews. He came to Jesus by night and said to him, 'Rabbi, we know that you are a teacher who has come from God; for no one can do these signs that you do apart from the presence of God.'

Psalm 26

Vindicate me, O Lord, for I have walked in my integrity,
and I have trusted in the Lord without wavering.
Prove me, O Lord, and try me; test my heart and mind.
For your steadfast love is before my eyes, and I walk in faithfulness
to you.

I do not sit with the worthless, nor do I consort with hypocrites;
I hate the company of evildoers, and will not sit with the wicked.
I wash my hands in innocence, and go around your altar, O Lord,
singing aloud a song of thanksgiving, and telling all your wondrous
deeds.

O Lord, I love the house in which you dwell, and the place where
your glory abides.
Do not sweep me away with sinners, nor my life with the
bloodthirsty,
those in whose hands are evil devices, and whose right hands are full
of bribes.
But as for me, I walk in my integrity; redeem me, and be gracious to
me.
My foot stands on level ground; in the great congregation I will bless
the Lord.

John 14:1-3

'Do not let your hearts be troubled. Believe in God, believe also in me. In my Father's house there are many dwelling places. If it were not so, would I have told you that I go to prepare a place for you? And if I go and prepare a place for you, I will come again and will take you to myself, so that where I am, there you may be also.

5   **CELEBRATION OF ADVENT**

Luke 12:35-38

Be dressed for action and have your lamps lit; be like those who are waiting for their master to return from the wedding banquet, so that they may open the door for him as soon as he comes and knocks. Blessed are those slaves whom the master finds alert when he comes; truly I tell you, he will fasten his belt and have them sit down to eat, and he will come and serve them. If he comes during the middle of the night, or near dawn, and finds them so, blessed are those slaves.

6   **SERVICE OF RECONCILIATION**

Colossians 3:12-15

As God's chosen ones, holy and beloved, clothe yourselves with compassion, kindness, humility, meekness, and patience. Bear with one another and, if anyone has a complaint against another, forgive each other; just as the Lord has forgiven you, so you also must forgive. Above all, clothe yourselves with love, which binds everything together in perfect harmony. And let the peace of Christ rule in your hearts, to which indeed you were called to one body. And be thankful.

Psalm 103:1-2, 3 and 8, 11-12

Bless the Lord, O my soul,
and all that is within me,
Bless his holy name.
Bless the Lord, O my soul,
and do not forget all his benefits-
who forgives all your iniquity,
who heals all your diseases...

The Lord is merciful and gracious,
slow to anger and abounding in steadfast love.
For as the heavens are high above the earth,
so great in his steadfast love
toward those who fear him;
as far as the east is from the west,
so far he removes our transgressions from us.

Matthew 3:1-6

In those days John the Baptist appeared in the wilderness of Judea proclaiming, 'Repent, for the kingdom of heaven has come near.' This is the one of whom the prophet Isaiah spoke when he said,

'The voice of one crying out in the wilderness:

"Prepare the way of the Lord, make his paths straight." '

Now John wore clothing of camel's hair with a leather belt around his waist, and his food was locusts and wild honey. Then the people of Jerusalem and all Judea were going out to him, and all the region along the Jordan, and they were baptised by him in the river Jordan, confessing their sins.

7 A CELEBRATION FOR THE NEW YEAR

Ecclesiastes 3:1-8

For everything there is a season, and a time for every matter under heaven:

a time to be born, and a time to die; a time to plant, and a time to pluck up what is planted;

a time to kill, and a time to heal; a time to break down, and a time to build up;

a time to weep, and a time to laugh; a time to mourn, and a time to dance;

a time to throw away stones, and a time to gather stones together; a time to embrace, and a time to refrain from embracing;

a time to seek, and a time to lose; a time to keep, and a time to throw away;

a time to tear; and a time to sew; a time to keep silence, and a time to speak;

a time to love, and a time to hate; a time for war, and a time for peace.

8 ST VALENTINE

1 John 4:7-12

A Samaritan woman came to draw water, and Jesus said to her, 'Give me a drink' (His disciples had gone to the city to buy food.) The Samaritan woman said to him, 'How is it that you, a Jew, ask a drink of me, a woman of Samaria?' (Jews do not share things in common with Samaritans.) Jesus answered her, 'If you knew the gift of God, and who it is that is saying to you, 'Give me a drink,' you would have asked him, and he would have given you living water.' The woman said to him, 'Sir, you have no bucket, and the well is deep. Where do you get that living water? Are you greater than our ancestor Jacob, who gave us the well, and with his sons and his flocks drank from it?'

Psalm 90:12, 14, 16-17

So teach us to count our days that we may gain a wise heart...

Satisfy us in the morning with your steadfast love,
so that we may rejoice and be glad all our days...

Let your work be manifest to your servants, and your glorious power to their children.

Let the favor of the Lord our God be upon us, and prosper for us the work of our hands-

O prosper the work of our hands!

John 3:16-17

'For God so loved the world that he gave his only Son, so that everyone who believes in him may not perish but may have eternal life. 'Indeed, God did not send the Son into the world to condemn the world, but in order that the world might be saved through him.

9   ASH WEDNESDAY – BLESSING AND DISTRIBUTION OF ASHES

Joel 2:12-18

Yet even now, says the Lord, return to me with all your heart, with fasting, with weeping, and with mourning; rend your hearts and not your clothing. Return to the Lord, your God, for he is gracious and merciful, slow to anger, and abounding in steadfast love, and relents from punishing. Who knows whether he will not turn and relent, and leave a blessing behind him, a grain offering and a drink offering for the Lord, your God?

Blow the trumpet in Zion; sanctify a fast; call a solemn assembly; gather the people. Sanctify the congregation; assemble the aged; gather the children, even infants at the breast. Let the bridegroom leave his room, and the bride her canopy.

Between the vestibule and the altar let the priests, the ministers of the Lord, weep. Let them say, 'Spare your people, O Lord, and do not make your heritage a mockery, a byword among the nations. Why should it be said among the peoples, "Where is their God?" '

Then the Lord became jealous for his land, and had pity on his people.

Psalm 51

Have mercy on me, O God,
according to your steadfast love;
according to your abundant mercy
blot out my transgressions.
Wash me thoroughly from my iniquity,
and cleanse me from my sin.

For I know my transgressions,
and my sin is ever before me.
Against you, you alone, have I sinned,
and done what is evil in your sight,
so that you are justified in your sentence
and blameless when you pass judgement.
Indeed, I was born guilty,
a sinner when my mother conceived me.

10 PENITENTIAL SERVICE – LENTEN SEASON

Isaiah 9:2-4, 6

The people who walked in darkness have seen a great light; those who lived in a land of deep darkness- on them light has shined. You have multiplied the nation, you have increased its joy; they rejoice before you as with joy at the harvest, as people exult when dividing plunder. For the yoke of their burden, and the bar across their shoulders, the rod of their oppressor, you have broken as on the day of Midian.

For a child has been born for us, a son given to us; authority rests upon his shoulders; and he named Wonderful Counselor, Mighty God, Everlasting Father, Prince of Peace.

11 SERVICE OF HEALING

James 5:13-16

Are any among you suffering? They should pray. Are any cheerful? They should sing songs of praise. Are any among you sick? They should call for the elders of the church and have them pray over them, anointing them with oil in the name of the Lord. The prayer of faith will save the sick, and the Lord will raise them up; and anyone who has committed sins will be forgiven. Therefore confess your sins to one another, and pray for one another, so that you may be healed. The prayer of the righteous is powerful and effective.

Psalm 25:4-5, 8-9, 10, 14, 15-16

Make me to know your ways, O Lord; teach me your paths.
Lead me in your truth, and teach me,
for you are the God of my salvation;
for you I wait all day long...

Good and upright is the Lord;
therefore he instructs sinners in the way.
He leads the humble in what is right and teaches the humble his
way.
All the paths of the Lord are steadfast love and faithfulness, for those
who keep his covenant and his decrees...

The friendship of the Lord is for those who fear him,
 and he makes his covenant known to them.
My eyes are ever toward the Lord,
for he will pluck my feet out of the net.

Turn to me and be gracious to me,
for I am lonely and afflicted.

Matthew 8: 14-17

When Jesus entered Peter's house, he saw his mother-in-law lying in
bed with a fever; he touched her hand, and the fever left her, and
she got up and began to serve him. That evening they brought to
him many who were possessed with demons; and he cast out the
spirits with a word, and cured all who were sick. This was to fulfill
what had been spoken through the prophet Isaiah, 'He took our
infirmities and bore our diseases.'

1 Timothy 2:1-4

First of all, then, I urge that supplications, prayers, intercessions, and thanksgivings be made for everyone, for kings and all who are in high position, so that we may lead a quiet and peaceable life in all godliness and dignity. This is right and is acceptable in the sight of God our Savior, who desires everyone to be saved and to come to the knowledge of truth.

Psalm 25:1-2, 4, 5, 6

To you O Lord, I lift up my soul.
O my God, in you I trust;
Do not let me be put to shame;
Do not let my enemies exult over me.

Make me know your ways, O Lord;
teach me your paths.
Lead me in your truth, and teach me,
for you are the God of my salvation;
for you I wait all day long.
Be mindful of your mercy, O Lord,
and of your steadfast love,
For they have been from of old.

Matthew 6:7-13

'When you are praying, do not heap up empty phrases as the Gentiles do; for they think that they will be heard because of their many words. Do not be like them, for your Father knows what you need before you ask him. Pray then in this way:

Our Father in heaven,
hallowed by your name.
Your kingdom come.
Your will be done,
on earth as it is in heaven.
Give us this day our daily bread.
And forgive us our debts,
as we also have forgiven our debtors.
And do not bring us to the time of trial,
but rescue us from the evil one.

13. A LITURGY FOR EXAMINATIONS

Ecclesiastes 11:7-10

Light is sweet, and it is pleasant for the eyes to see the sun. Even those who live many years should rejoice in them all; yet let them remember that the days of darkness will be many. All that comes is vanity. Rejoice, young man, while you are young, and let your heart cheer you in the days of your youth. Follow the inclination of your heart and the desire of your eyes, but know that for all these things God will bring you into judgement. Banish anxiety from your mind, and put away pain from your body; for youth and the dawn of life are vanity.

14. A LITURGY TO MARK THE END OF THE SCHOOL YEAR

Philippians 4:4-9

Rejoice in the Lord always; again I will say, Rejoice. Let your gentleness be known to everyone. The Lord is near. Do not worry about anything, but in everything by prayer and supplication with thanksgiving let your requests be made known to God. And the peace of God, which surpasses all understanding, will guard your hearts and your minds in Christ Jesus.

Finally, beloved, whatever is true, whatever is honourable, whatever is just, whatever is pure, whatever is pleasing, whatever is commendable, if there is any excellence and if there is anything worthy of praise, think about these things. Keep on doing the things that you have learned and received and heard and seen in me, and the God of peace will be with you.

Psalm 150:1-2, 3-4, 5-6

Praise the Lord! Praise God in his sanctuary;
praise him in his mighty firmament!
Praise him for his mighty deeds;
praise him according to his surpassing greatness!

Praise him with trumpet sound;
praise him with lute and harp!
Praise him with tambourine and dance;
praise him with strings and pipe!
Praise him with clanging cymbals;
praise him with loud clashing cymbals!
Let everything that breathes praise the Lord!
Praise the Lord!

John 15:12-17

'This is my commandment, that you love one another as I have loved you. No one has greater love than this, to lay down one's life for one's friends. You are my friends if you do what I command you. I do not call you servants any longer, because the servant does not know what the master is doing; but I have called you friends, because I have made known to you everything that I have heard from my Father. You did not choose me but I chose you. And I appointed you to go and bear fruit, fruit that will last, so that the Father will give you whatever you ask him in my name. I am giving you these commands so that you may love one another.

15 A GRADUATION LITURGY

Ecclesiastes 3:1-8

For everything there is a season, and a time for every matter under heaven:
a time to be born, and a time to die; a time to plant, and a time to pluck up what is planted;
a time to kill, and a time to heal; a time to break down, and a time to build up;
a time to weep, and a time to laugh; a time to mourn, and a time to dance;
a time to throw away stones, and a time to gather stones together; a time to embrace, and a time to refrain from embracing;
a time to seek, and a time to lose; a time to keep, and a time to throw away;
a time to tear; and a time to sew; a time to keep silence, and a time to speak;
a time to love, and a time to hate; a time for war, and a time for peace.

Psalm 113:1-2, 3-4, 5-6

Praise the Lord!
Praise, O servants of the Lord;
praise the name of the Lord.
Blessed be the name of the Lord
from this time on and forevermore.
From the rising of the sun to its setting
the name of the Lord is to be praised.
The Lord is high above all nations,
and his glory above the heavens.

Who is like the Lord our God, who is seated on high,
who looks far down on the heavens and the earth?

Philippians 4:4-7

Rejoice in the Lord always; again I will say, Rejoice. Let your gentleness be known to everyone. The Lord is near. Do not worry about anything, but in everything by prayer and supplication with thanksgiving let your requests be made known to God. And the peace of God, which surpasses all understanding, will guard your hearts and your minds in Christ Jesus.

Luke 24:13-39

Now on that same day two of them were going to a village called Emmaus, about seven miles from Jerusalem, and talking with each other about all these things that had happened. While they were talking and discussing, Jesus himself came near and went with them, but their eyes were kept from recognizing him. And he said to them, 'What are you discussing with each other while you walk along?' They stood still, looking sad. Then one of them, whose name was

Cleopas, answered him, 'Are you the only stranger in Jerusalem who does not know the things that have taken place there in these days?' He asked them, 'What things?' They replied, 'The things about Jesus of Nazareth, who was a prophet mighty in deed and word before God and all the people, and how our chief priests and leaders handed him over to be condemned to death and crucified him. But we had hoped that he was the one to redeem Israel. Yes, and besides all this, it is now the third day since these things took place. More over, some women of our group astounded us. They were at the tomb early this morning, and when they did not find his body there, they came back and told us that they had indeed seen a vision of angels who said that he was alive. Some of those who were with us went to the tomb and found it just as the women had said; but they did not see him.' Then he said to them, 'Oh, how foolish you are and how slow of heart to believe all that the prophets have declared! Was it not necessary that the Messiah should suffer these things and then enter into his glory?' Then beginning with Moses and all the prophets, he interpreted to them the things about himself in all the scriptures.

As they came near the village to which they were going, he walked ahead as if he were going on. But they urged him strongly, saying, 'Stay with us, because it is almost evening and the day is now nearly over.' So he went in to stay with them. When he was at the table with them, he took bread, blessed and broke it, and gave it to them. Then their eyes were opened, and they recognized him; and he vanished from their sight. They said to each other, 'Were not our hearts burning within us while he was talking to us on the road, while he was opening the scriptures to us?' That same hour they got up and returned to Jerusalem; and they found the eleven and their companions gathered together. They were saying 'The Lord has risen indeed, and he has appeared to Simon!' Then they told what had happened on the road, and how he had been made known to them in the breaking of the bread. While they were talking about this,

Jesus himself stood among them and said to them, 'Peace be with you.' They were startled and terrified, and thought they were seeing a ghost. He said to them, 'Why are you frightened, and why do doubts arise in your hearts? Look at my hands and my feet; see that it is I myself. Touch me and see; for a ghost does not have flesh and bones as you see that I have.'